THE HORSE

A SMALL APPRECIATION

Macdonald Illustrated

A Macdonald Illustrated book

First published by Pocknell & Co in April 1991

First issued in Great Britain by Macdonald Illustrated
a division of
Macdonald & Co (Publishers) Ltd
Orbit House
1 New Fetter Lane
London EC4A 1AR

A member of Maxwell Macmillan Pergamon Publishing Corporation

Designed by Pocknell
Jacket sketch by Sir Alfred Munnings
Produced by Lennard Associates Ltd,
Mackerye End, Harpenden, Herts

Printed in Great Britain by
Ebenezer Baylis & Son Ltd, Worcester
Bound in Scotland by Hunter and Foulis, Edinburgh
Typeset by Paragraph Typesetting, Witham

A CIP catalogue record for this book is available
from the British Library

ISBN 0 356 20268 2

We owe so much to the horse, more than we sometimes admit. This Small Appreciation, full of good-humoured variety in text and pictures, is a reminder of our many partnerships - in farm work, with carriages and carts, riding for pleasure, racing and the equestrian sports - horses have helped to smooth our path and make our history.

Captain Mark Phillips CVO

Chairman of the British Equestrian Olympic Fund

I heard a horseman
Ride over the hill;
The moon shone clear,
The night was still;
His helm was silver,
And pale was he;
And the horse he rode
Was of ivory.

Walter de la Mare *The Horseman*

So the whole morning he runs here, fulfilling the track
Of so many suns: vanishing the mole's way, moving
Into mole's mysteries under the zodiac,
Racing, stopping in the circle. Startled he stands
Dazzled, where darkness is green, where the sunlight is black,
While his mother, grazing, is moving away
From the lagging star of those stars, the unrisen wonder
In the path of the dead, fallen from the sun in her hooves
And eluding the dead hands, begging him to play.

VERNON WATKINS *FOAL*

William Nicholson

I do not think I ever enjoyed any period of my life so much as those pleasant meetings at Newmarket; for we did the thing 'proper'... An hour or so before the races we mounted our fresh hacks, and with a fly to carry our coats, cloaks and convey our two grooms, we caracoled down to the races, seldom dismounting, but riding from saddling-paddock to betting ring, and backwards and forwards between different courses. If it rained real hard, we hopped into our fly... Ah! those were happy days and no error.

SIR JOHN ASTLEY *FIFTY YEARS OF MY LIFE*

Sir Alfred Munnings

Under starter's orders, Newmarket, cries of 'No, no, sir'

Sophie's first love is Sammy. He is a 12 hh Thelwellian grey with hairy heels and thick eyelashes fringeing his innocent blue eyes. With hoots of laughter his parents enter him for classes filled with glossy show ponies ridden by children in washable coats, rubber riding boots and new blue hats. Sophie has jodhpur boots and a tweed coat recently shaken out of moth-balls, belonging to her mother. She and Sammy have to be dragged into the ring and once there he refuses to do anything he is told. If he catches sight of Caroline he makes a dash for her, diving under the ropes and throwing Sophie on to her back in the mud. Sammy is wilful, wicked, stubborn, stupid, lazy and lovable. 'Sammy is a Pig.' Sophie adores him and dreams of bending-races and rosettes.

Ann Barr and Peter York

The Official Sloane Ranger Handbook

Alice M Coats

Everybody can see that the people who hunt are the right people, and the people who don't are the wrong ones.

BERNARD SHAW *HEARTBREAK HOUSE*

T Blinks

And now: on the field that I see night's darkness lies.
A brook brawls near: there are stars in the empty skies.
The grass is deep, and dense. As I push my way,
From sour-nettled ditch sweeps fragrance of clustering May.
I come to a stile. And lo, on the further side,
With still, umbrageous, night-clad fronds, spread wide,
A giant cedar broods. And in crescent's gleam -
A horse, milk-pale, sleek-shouldered, engendered of dream!
Startled, it lifts its muzzle, deep eyes agaze,
Silk-plaited mane... 'Whose pastures are thine to graze?
Creature, delicate, lovely, with womanlike head,
Sphinx-like, gazelle-like? Where tarries thy rider?' I said.

WALTER DE LA MARE *To KM*

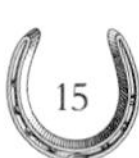

TONY EVANS

Another 'charming' brute attracted my attention... The 'sweetest little park horse that ever was crossed' was of course the 'very thing I wanted'. I thought so too; but the good nature of the dealer saved my pocket, whatever might be his good intentions; I was allowed to make trial of him. We danced a quadrille together with every gentleman and lady that we met mounted in Hyde Park, and I soon found that the lovely creature was better suited to Almack's than to me.

He *passaged* away in style by the band of the Guards, till every soldier grinned a salute, and no rhetoric of mine could divert him from his obvious purpose of escorting them to the palace. Once indeed, I prevailed on him to turn his head, but it was only to *passage* the other way, with his rump instead of his face to the troops. At last in sheer desperation, I plunged both spurs in him at once; he gave a spring that would have cleared a horse and gig, and then fairly bolted; running at speed to his stables again! I would as soon fondle a mad dog as take such another dance with a dandy!

SIR GEORGE STEPHEN

THE ADVENTURES OF A GENTLEMAN IN SEARCH OF A HORSE

Feliks Topolski *This England*

THE HORSE

Those lumbering horses in the steady plough,
On the bare field - I wonder why, just now,
They seemed terrible, so wild and strange,
Like magic power on the stony grange.

Perhaps some childish hour has come again,
When I watched fearful, through the blackening rain,
Their hooves like pistons in an ancient mill
Move up and down, yet seem as standing still.

Their conquering hooves which trod the stubble down
Were ritual that turned the field to brown,
And their great hulks were seraphim of gold,
Or mute ecstatic monsters on the mould.

And oh the rapture, when, one furrow done,
They marched broad-breasted to the sinking sun!
The light flowed off their bossy sides in flakes;
The furrows rolled behind like struggling snakes.

But when at dusk with steaming nostrils home
They came, they seemed gigantic in the gloam,
And warm and glowing with mysterious fire
That lit their smouldering bodies in the mire.

EDWIN MUIR *HORSES*

Clare Leighton *Ploughing*

Scores, hundreds of horses are wandering around,
gathering into herds
and into twos and threes,
lost, exhausted, bony, but still alive where they have been
able to wrench themselves free from a team whose
other horses have been killed;
some, like our horse, are still in harness,
or dragging a shaft with them,
or there is a pair with a broken draught-bar between
them...
and there are wounded horses...
the undecorated, unnamed heroes of the battle who for a
hundred, two hundred miles have hauled
this artillery, now dead and drowning in the swamp...
and all that ammunition, ammunition-limbers with their
chains...

ALEXANDER SOLZHENITSYN *AUGUST 1914*

F MATANIA *'GOOD-BYE, OLD MAN'*

Of course riding-off forms one and a very important means of preventing the opposite Back getting the ball. There are, however, two other ways, so often neglected, which are just as important. One is, to *hook the stick of the Back* whenever within reach. A little practice will enable a player to strike the stick of a man about to hit a back-hander, or if he does not swing it, but pushes it up, it may be hooked over his shoulder.

General Sir Beauvoir De Lisle *Tournament Polo*

Maurice Tulloch

Still Parvo had his foibles. He was a resolute, headstrong animal, that would go his own way in spite of all the pulling and hauling in the world. If he took it into his obstinate head to turn into a particular field, into it he would be; or against the gate-post he would bump the rider's leg in a way that would make him remember the difference of opinion between them. His was not a fiery, hot-headed spirit, with object or reason for its guide, but just a regular downright pig-headed sort of stupidity, that nobody could account for. He had a mouth like a bull, and would walk clean through a gate sometimes rather than be at the trouble of rising to leap it; at other times he would hop over it like a bird.

R S Surtees *Mr Sponge's Sporting Tour*

PHILIP BLACKER *FIRST TIME ON LONG REINS*

The ability and intelligence of the Suffolk horse is remarkable and, to a beginner like me, reassuring. Prince was able to walk the length of the furrow, between the growing potatoes, and when he was done you might never guess that he had passed that way, so sure and careful was every footfall.

PAUL HEINEY *PULLING PUNCHES*

HARRY BECKER

Peter and Santa saw the second house from the artistes' entrance. They slipped through the curtain at the side and crawled under the seats and watched from there. It was a lovely view, because they could see the artistes as well where they waited for their entrances. They had already learnt from Gus that every artiste had to be waiting to go into the ring two acts before their own... But what they did not know was what went on in the artistes' entrance. Most of the time they found it more enthralling than what was happening in the ring.

NOEL STREATFIELD *THE CIRCUS IS COMING*

PETER BLAKE

Three jolly gentlemen
In coats of red,
Rode their horses
Up to bed.

Three jolly gentlemen
Snored till morn,
Their horses champing
The golden corn.

Three jolly gentlemen,
At break of day,
Came clitter-clatter down the stairs
And galloped away.

WALTER DE LA MARE *THE HUNTSMEN*

William Nicholson

I have seen flowers come in stony places
And kind things done by men with ugly faces,
And the gold cup won by the worst horse at the races.
So I trust, too.

JOHN MASEFIELD *AN EPILOGUE*

LOWES DALBIAC LUARD *RACING STUDY*

Early next morning at the spring of day
Up rose our Host and roused us like a cock,
Gathering us together in a flock,
And off we rode at slightly faster pace
Than walking to St Thomas' watering-place;
And there our Host drew up, began to ease
His horse, and said, 'Now, listen if you please,
My lords! Remember what you promised me.
If evensong and mattins will agree
Let's see who shall be first to tell a tale.
And as I hope to drink good wine and ale
I'll be your judge. The rebel who disobeys,
However much the journey costs, he pays.
Now draw for cut and then we can depart;
The man who draws the shortest cut shall start.

CHAUCER *CANTERBURY TALES*

Elisabeth Frink

'It's true, you can get your drilling done earlier with horses. I drilled a piece of grass seed into this barley out here for that reason - with horses because it was so bad on the headland where I had to turn. If I'd ha' done it with a tractor I'd ha' chewed all the barley up.'

JOHN UTTING OF METTINGHAM, IN GEORGE EWART EVANS

HORSE POWER AND MAGIC

Harry Becker

On the last Wednesday in November, a steeplechase - the parties undertaking to surmount all obstructions, and to pursue in their progress as straight a line as possible. This contest lay between Mr Bullivant of Shroxton, Mr Day of Wymondham and Mr Frisby of Waltham, and was for a sweepstakes of one hundred guineas staked by each. They started from Womack's Lodge at half past twelve (the riders attired in handsome jockey dresses of orange, crimson, and sky-blue) to run round Woodal Head and back again, a distance somewhat exceeding eight miles.

Sporting Magazine (1804)

Henry Alken

We would like to thank all the generous contributors to this book.

Permissions have been received from the following publishers and authors' representatives and we are indebted to them for their promptness.

'Good-bye, old man' by F. Matania reproduced by permission of the Imperial War Museum.

'Racing Study' by Lowes Dalbiac Luard and two horses by Alice M. Coats reproduced by permission of The Michael Parkin Gallery.

'The Huntsmen', 'The Horseman' and 'To KM' reproduced by permission of the Literary Trustees of Walter de la Mare and the Society of Authors as their representative.

Select verses from 'Horses' by Edwin Muir and 'The Foal' by Vernon Watkins reproduced by permission of Faber and Faber Ltd.

'First time on long reins' by Philip Blacker reproduced by permission of Mr Douglas Bunn.

Prue Loftus for allowing us to reproduce the Harry Becker drawings used as end papers.

Etching by Elisabeth Frink.

'August 1914' by Alexander Solzhenitsyn by permission of Bodley Head.

'The Circus is Coming' by Noel Streatfield published by Dent and Sons.

'Pulling Punches' by Paul Heiney reproduced by permission of AP Watt.

We apologise to those people whom we have been unable to trace for permission before going to print.